# POLAR VORTEX

## CLIMATE CHANGE AND ITS EFFECTS

Virginia Loh-Hagan

# 45TH PARALLEL PRESS

Published in the United States of America by Cherry Lake Publishing
Ann Arbor, Michigan
www.cherrylakepublishing.com

Reading Adviser: Beth Walker Gambro, MS, Ed., Reading Consultant, Yorkville, IL
Cover Designer: Felicia Macheske

Photo Credits: © justoomm/Shutterstock.com, cover, 1; © justoomm/Shutterstock.com, 5; © Elena Elisseeva/
Shutterstock.com, 6; © Meyta/Shutterstock.com, 9; ©/Nick Starichenko/Shutterstock.com, 11, 12; © Ipedan/
Shutterstock.com, 17; © Zoran Ras/Shutterstock.com, 18; © Vadym Zaitsev/Shutterstock.com, 21; © Alan Budman/
Shutterstock.com, 22; © Marouansitti/Shutterstock.com, 24; © Roschetzky Photography/Shutterstock.com, 25;
© C. R. Gette/Shutterstock.com, 29

Graphic Elements Throughout: © Chipmunk131/Shutterstock.com; © Nowik Sylwia/Shutterstock.com;
© Andrey_Popov/Shutterstock.com; © NadzeyaShanchuk/Shutterstock.com; © KathyGold/Shutterstock.com;
© Black creator/Shutterstock.com; © Edvard Molnar/Shutterstock.com; © Elenadesign/Shutterstock.com;
© estherpoon/Shutterstock.com

**45th Parallel Press** is an imprint of Cherry Lake Publishing.

Library of Congress Cataloging-in-Publication Data
Names: Loh-Hagan, Virginia, author.
Title: Polar vortex : climate change and its effects / by Virginia Loh-Hagan.
Description: Ann Arbor, Michigan : Cherry Lake Publishing, 2022. | Series: Behind the curtain
Identifiers: LCCN 2021037493 | ISBN 9781534199491 (hardcover) | ISBN 9781668900635 (paperback) |
    ISBN 9781668906392 (ebook) | ISBN 9781668902073 (pdf)
Subjects: LCSH: Polar vortex—Juvenile literature. | Climatic changes—Juvenile literature.
Classification: LCC QC994.75 .L64 2022 | DDC 551.50911/3—dc23
LC record available at https://lccn.loc.gov/2021037493

Cherry Lake Publishing would like to acknowledge the work of the Partnership for 21st Century Learning,
a Network of Battelle for Kids. Please visit *http://www.battelleforkids.org/networks/p21* for more information.

Printed in the United States of America
Corporate Graphics

## A Note on Dramatic Retellings

Participating in Readers Theater, or dramatic retellings, can greatly improve reading skills, especially fluency. The books in the **BEHIND THE CURTAIN** series give readers opportunities to learn about important historical events in a fun and engaging way. These books serve as a bridge to more complex texts. All the characters and stories have been fictionalized. To learn more, check out the Perspectives Library series and the Modern Perspectives series, as **BEHIND THE CURTAIN** books are aligned to these stories.

# TABLE of CONTENTS

# HISTORICAL BACKGROUND

The polar vortex is always around. It's cold air that hovers around the poles. Earth has north and south poles. These areas are extremely cold.

The polar vortex is a large area of cold air. This air is low pressure. It swirls around. That's why it's called a vortex. The air flows counterclockwise. This keeps colder air near the poles. It also keeps warmer air in the south.

The polar vortex is there all year long. But it's stronger during the winter. During winter, the polar vortex may grow. Arctic air may escape. It may push down south. Cold surges are common. But extreme surges are not.

## Vocabulary

**hovers** (HUH-vuhrz) remains in one place in the air

**counterclockwise** (kown-tuhr-KLOK-wyz) moving opposite of the movement of hands on a clock

**surges** (SUHR-juhz) sudden powerful forward or upward movements

# FLASH FACT!

*As temperatures warmed, the risk of floods increased.*

## Vocabulary

**exposed** (ik-SPOZD)
not covered or hidden; visible

**frostbite** (FROST-byte)
damage to body tissues from freezing,
which can result in loss of limbs

**hypothermia**
(hye-poh-THUHR-mee-uh) a dangerous
drop in body temperature
that could lead to death

In 2014, North America experienced extreme weather. Canada and the United States suffered. There was a lot of snowfall and freezing rains. Lakes froze over. There were super-cold temperatures. Subzero wind chills were common.

Around 250 million Americans were affected in some way. Shipping and airline flights stopped. Roads became dangerous. People couldn't get supplies. They lost power. They didn't have heat. Schools and businesses closed. Going outside for as little as 5 minutes could cause harm. Exposed skin could freeze. This causes frostbite. Some people got hypothermia. More than 20 people died.

There have been other cold waves. There will be more cold waves. Extreme weather is here to stay.

# CAST of CHARACTERS

**NARRATOR:** person who helps tells the story

**JACK:** a young student living in 2014; Sarah's older brother

**BETH:** the mother of Jack and Sarah

**SARAH:** a young student living in 2014 and a college student in 2021; Jack's younger sister

**KENNY:** a college student living in 2021; Sarah's classmate

# SPOTLIGHT
## AMPLIFICATION OF AN ACTIVIST

Mai Nguyen is a climate researcher. She's also a farmer. She's known as Farmer Mai. She studies the atmosphere and the soil. She studies ways humans are destroying Earth. Her family are Vietnamese refugees. Refugees escaped from war. Nguyen wanted to help refugees settle in the United States. She wanted to help the planet. She started community gardens, food pantries, and farmers' markets. Nguyen wanted people to have access to healthy foods. She also wanted people of color to have access to cultural foods. She said, "That's why I farm: to provide delicious, nutritious, culturally appropriate food using environmentally beneficial methods. It's critical to ensuring food security and good health for *everyone.*" She thinks the 2 big issues today are climate change and social inequality.

## FLASH FACT!

*The polar vortex was first discovered in the 1850s. The term became popular in 2014.*

# ACT 1

**NARRATOR:** *The 2014 polar vortex storm has hit. It's January 6, 2014. It's the coldest day of the storm.* **JACK** *is stuck at home. He's with his mother,* **BETH***, and sister* **SARAH***. They're in Chicago, Illinois.*

**JACK:** It's so cold in here. Are you sure the heat is on?

**BETH:** Yes, it's on. But everyone is using heat right now. There's only so much power. I hope we don't have a **power outage**. That would be awful.

**JACK:** I'm wearing 3 layers of clothes.

**BETH:** Here's an extra blanket.

**SARAH:** Why don't we use the fireplace?

**BETH:** We ran out of wood. We can't get more. It's too cold to go out. It's dangerous out there. We could freeze to death!

**JACK:** When is Dad getting home?

**Vocabulary**
**power outage** (POW-uhr OW-tij)
the loss of electricity in a given area for a given amount of time

*FLASH FACT!*

*In Chicago, 2014 is known as the "year of the polar vortex."*

**BETH:** He'll come as soon as he can. He's stuck on the roads.

**JACK:** How is he staying warm?

**BETH:** City leaders turned buses into warming **shelters**. They're picking up homeless and **stranded** people. I hope your dad found one of those buses.

**SARAH:** Why is this happening?

**JACK:** It's because of the polar vortex.

**SARAH:** What's that?

**JACK:** It's a bunch of cold air. Imagine air spinning in a bowl. The bowl is the North Pole. This air is always spinning.

**SARAH:** The spinning sounds bad. I wish it would stop.

**JACK:** The vortex is spinning. Actually, the spinning is good. It traps the cold air in the bowl. It keeps it at the North Pole.

**BETH:** Sometimes cold air escapes. That's what's happening right now.

**SARAH:** If it's good, why is it freezing cold?

**Vocabulary**
**shelters** (SHEL-tuhrz)
places that provide safety
**stranded** (STRAN-duhd)
left behind

*FLASH FACT!*
*Warming shelters are usually community centers such as schools or libraries. They provide food and a warm place to stay.*

**BETH:** We're feeling the effects of the escaped cold air.

**SARAH:** But how did the air escape in the first place?

**JACK:** The vortex got weak. Trapped air spilled out. It spread out. It crept down to us. We're feeling patches of cold air.

**SARAH:** What made the vortex weak?

**JACK:** Some scientists blame global warming.

**SARAH:** What's global warming? Is it a good or bad thing?

**JACK:** Global warming is a bad thing. It's the long-term heating of Earth's **climate**. Heat gets trapped in Earth's **atmosphere**. This causes hot temperatures. It causes rising sea levels.

**BETH:** Look outside. There's nothing warm going on. It's cold. These climate change **theories** are confusing.

# SPOTLIGHT
## A SPECIAL EFFECT

Preppers are people who prepare for disasters. They collect supplies needed for living. They store all these things. Some have underground bunkers. Preppers have enough supplies to last a long period of time. Most preppers are survivalists. They know how to grow their own food and hunt wild animals. In 2020, the COVID-19 pandemic broke out. In the early days, people were unprepared and scared. They scrambled to get basic things. For example, many people bought and hoarded toilet paper. This caused shortages. But preppers didn't need to shop. They had everything already. Prepping is a way to control uncertain futures.

### Vocabulary

**climate** (KLY-muht) the average weather conditions in an area over a long period of time

**atmosphere** (AT-muh-sfihr) the envelope of gases surrounding Earth

**theories** (THEE-reez) ideas used to explain something

## FLASH FACT!

*Scientists study weather. They use satellites. They predict weather.*

**SARAH:** I'm confused too. It's super cold outside. It's not warm at all.

**JACK:** Remember how there's ice at the poles?

**SARAH:** Like icebergs and **glaciers**?

**JACK:** That's right. As the planet warms, this ice melts. This raises sea levels. The waters get warmer. Extra water **evaporates**. It goes into the air. This causes more warming.

**SARAH:** I see. The melting makes the vortex weak. This makes our winters colder and harsher.

**BETH:** The climate changes. Temperatures go up. They go down. It's been like this forever. This is nothing new.

**JACK:** But something is definitely happening. Remember that TV show about Glacier National Park? In 1910, there were 150 glaciers. Today, it has fewer than 30.

**SARAH:** I remember watching that. It said sea levels could rise more than 6 feet (1.8 meters).

**Vocabulary**

**glaciers** (GLAY-shuhrz)
slowly moving masses of ice

**evaporates** (ih-VA-puh-raytes)
turns from liquid into vapor

**FLASH FACT!**

*The polar vortex is also called an Arctic hurricane or Arctic cyclone.*

**JACK:** Islands will be underwater. Beaches and cities could disappear.

**BETH:** This is starting to sound like one of your science-fiction movies. Some people think climate change is a joke. We're going to be fine.

**JACK:** We can be fine. We just have to take better care of our planet.

**SARAH:** How can we do that?

**JACK:** We can save energy. Using gas, oil, and coal releases gases. These gases are called **greenhouse gases**. They collect in our atmosphere. They work like a thick blanket. They trap the sun's heat.

**SARAH:** I learned about this in school! We talked about **reducing**. We talked about **reusing**. We talked about **recycling**.

**BETH:** I can get behind all those things. It saves us money!

**SARAH:** And it helps the environment.

**Vocabulary**

**greenhouse gases** (GREEN-hows GA-suhz) gases in Earth's atmosphere that trap heat

**reducing** (rih-DOO-sing) the process of using less

**reusing** (ree-YOO-zing) the process of using again

**recycling** (ree-SYE-kling) the process of turning trash into new products

*FLASH FACT!*

*Extreme weather is a popular movie theme.*

# ACT 2

**NARRATOR:** *It's 7 years later on February 15, 2021. There's another polar vortex storm.* **SARAH** *is in college. She's in Texas. Sarah and her friend* **KENNY** *are in the college library.*

**SARAH:** I can't believe this is happening again.

**KENNY:** Again?

**SARAH:** I was in Chicago in 2014. That's when I learned about the polar vortex.

**KENNY:** I remember reading about that storm. That was the first time I heard that word.

**SARAH:** I was stuck in the house for 5 days. It was so cold.

**KENNY:** That sounds awful.

**SARAH:** The only good thing was being able to spend time with my family. My brother had studied the polar vortex in school. He had told me a lot about it. It sparked my interest.

**KENNY:** Is that why you're studying science?

## FLASH FACT!

Many people posted winter storm pictures on social media.

**Vocabulary**
**politician** (pah-luh-TIH-shuhn)
a leader in government

## FLASH FACT!

*The spinning is also known as a jet stream. It's a very strong wind. It's above Earth's surface.*

**SARAH:** Yes. I want to be a climate scientist.

**KENNY:** That's great. We need more scientists. I want to be a **politician**.

**SARAH:** We need politicians too. You need to help fight global warming. You can do this by passing good laws. You can do this by convincing people of climate change.

**KENNY:** It's amazing how many people don't believe in climate change.

**SARAH:** We're in Texas. It's not supposed to snow here. I moved here to avoid snow!

**KENNY:** What exactly is the polar vortex?

**SARAH:** I asked my brother the same thing. I see the polar vortex as a spinning top. It spins at the top of our planet. Sometimes, a strong energy wave hits it. Cold air breaks loose. It heads our way.

**KENNY:** So, is it normal?

**SARAH:** The polar vortex is totally normal. What's not normal is how far south the storms have traveled. It's cold in places that should be warm.

**KENNY:** There seem to be more extreme winter storms. These storms are also more severe. Why is that?

**SARAH:** Scientists are still not exactly sure. It could just be weather doing its thing. Or it could be human activities causing climate change. Or it could be both.

**TEXAS**

## FLASH FACT!

*Texas is more known for heat waves, not snow.*

**KENNY:** Extreme weather is everywhere. The news said it was warmer in Alaska than here. It also said Florida was too hot. The heat caused plants to bloom early.

**SARAH:** Nature is telling us something.

**KENNY:** Hopefully, this storm will pass soon.

**SARAH:** I think there's more to come. Prepare yourself.

**NARRATOR:** *It's 5 days later.* **JACK** *lives in California.* **SARAH** *left Texas and is at Jack's house. She and Jack are talking.*

**JACK:** I'm glad you're safe from the storm. It's like the polar vortex is following you.

**SARAH:** I had no choice but to come here. I can't live in my house anymore. The **power grid** failed. I lost electricity.

**JACK:** Your house must have been freezing.

**SARAH:** It gets worse. Even when the power came back, I didn't have running water. City leaders told us to boil any water we did have.

**JACK:** You can't live without water.

**SARAH:** Then my neighbor's water pipes burst. There was flooding everywhere. Things were bad.

# SPOTLIGHT

## EXTRA! EXTRA! BONUS FACT!

The coldest place on Earth is the Eastern Antarctic Plateau. Plateaus are high landforms shaped like tables. The Eastern Antarctic Plateau is a frozen ice ridge in Antarctica. Antarctica is one of Earth's seven continents. It covers Earth's South Pole. Data was collected between 2004 and 2016. The Eastern Antarctic Plateau has the lowest temperature ever recorded on Earth at –144 degrees Fahrenheit (–98 degrees Celsius). It's as cold as it can possibly get on Earth. It's a cold desert. The only humans in the area work at the Dome Fuji Station. This station was built in 1995. It's a Japanese research center. Japanese scientists drilled ice cores. Ice cores are cylinders of ice. The scientists studied air bubbles in each layer of fallen snow. The ice is believed to be more than 720,000 years old.

**Vocabulary**
**power grid** (POW-uhr GRID)
a network of power lines and equipment used to send electricity over an area

## FLASH FACT!

More than 4.5 million Texas homes and businesses were left without power.

**JACK:** Luckily, you were able to come here.

**SARAH:** I'm definitely lucky. But many other people aren't. They weren't able to **evacuate**. They're stuck in freezing homes without food and water.

**JACK:** On top of that, we're dealing with the COVID-19 **virus**.

**SARAH:** The winter storms delayed delivery of **vaccines**.

**JACK:** That makes sense. Roads are iced over. Trucks can't get there. I heard stores are out of everything.

**SARAH:** I'm most worried about hospitals. Hospitals are having a hard time caring for patients.

**JACK:** Can you imagine a hospital not having water? That is tough.

**SARAH:** About 200 people have died. Some died from hypothermia. Some from house fires. Some from drownings. Some from car crashes.

**JACK:** Extreme weather is not a joke. I'm glad you want to be a scientist.

**SARAH:** We can all do our part. We can fight climate change together.

**Vocabulary**

**evacuate** (ih-VA-kyoo-wayt) to escape from a place of danger to a safer place

**virus** (VYE-rus) a type of germ that can make people sick; a virus caused the COVID-19 disease

**vaccines** (VAK-seenz) medicines that protect people from germs, viruses, and diseases

**FLASH FACT!**

Many people helped Texans in need. They provided food and supplies.

# FLASH FORWARD
## CURRENT CONNECTIONS

*The polar vortex* happened in 2014. But its legacy lives on. We are still feeling its effects. There is still so much work for us to do.

**Stop climate change:** Focus on saving energy. Energy is used to grow and transport food. Eat foods that are grown locally and are in season. Another thing you can do is to stop using single-use plastic. These plastic products are used once and thrown away. Examples include plastic bags and eating utensils. It takes a lot of energy to make these products.

**Protect all members of our community:** It's important to care for others. Elderly and homeless people suffer the most in extreme weather. Elderly people have weaker immune systems. It's harder for them to fight sickness. Make sure they're in safe places. Make sure they have their medicines. Homeless people don't have shelter. They're exposed to harsh weather conditions. Support shelters and food banks. Most cities have a hotline. People can call this phone number to get help for homeless people.

**Know about power outages:** We use power for almost everything we do. We use power to cook. We use power for light. We use power for our devices. Not having power disrupts our lives. For most, power outages are inconvenient. But for some, power outages are life-threatening. Some people need machines to breathe. Without power, they'll die. Write to power companies. Write to city leaders. Make sure power grids support hospitals. Make sure they support other community centers. These places need to be served first.

# CONSIDER THIS!

**TAKE A POSITION!** Most scientists believe climate change is real. Some Americans do not. Do you think climate change exists or not? Argue your point with reasons and evidence.

**SAY WHAT?** Has anyone you know experienced extreme weather? Interview them. Describe what you learned.

**THINK ABOUT IT!** Study the weather patterns in your area. Have you noticed anything odd? Has it been getting hotter or colder? Are there more storms? Think about the reasons for the weather changes.

## Learn More

Gilles, Renae. *Climate Change in Infographics.* Ann Arbor, MI: Cherry Lake Publishing, 2021.

Herman, Gail. *What Is Climate Change?* New York, NY: Penguin Workshop, 2018.

Labrecque, Ellen. *Climate Change.* Ann Arbor, MI: Cherry Lake Publishing, 2017.

Orr, Tamra B. *Polar Vortex and Climate Change.* Ann Arbor, MI: Cherry Lake Publishing, 2017.

# INDEX

## ABOUT THE AUTHOR

Dr. Virginia Loh-Hagan is an author, former K–8 teacher, curriculum designer, and university professor. She's currently the director of the Asian Pacific Islander Desi American (APIDA) Center at San Diego State University. She has experienced heat waves and wildfires. She believes climate change exists. She lives in San Diego with her one very tall husband and two very naughty dogs.